Out Of The Office: Making The Transition To Working From Home

Maya Middlemiss

Copyright © 2020 Maya Middlemiss

All rights reserved.

ISBN: 979-856-1-74-4525

Contents

Introduction _____ 1
   How to use this book series _____ 3
   Is the Healthy Happy Homeworking series for you? _____ 4
   No "business in a box", or even in a book _____ 5

Chapter One - Flipping expectations: from the exception to the new normality _____ 7
   Unexamined assumptions overturned _____ 8
   Then suddenly, everything changed… _____ 12
   But *this* is not what I meant! _____ 15

Chapter Two — The reluctant homeworker _____ 20
   Saved time _____ 23
   Saved money _____ 25
   Saved communities _____ 26
   A Saved Planet _____ 29
   Saved making a choice..? _____ 30

Chapter Three — Employment or entrepreneurship? _____ 34
   Remote jobs: Default or orientation? _____ 36
   Decoding the remote job advertisement _____ 38
   Remote-first roles _____ 39
   How remote can you be? _____ 41
   Always on? _____ 42

What's your side of the deal? _____ 43

Chapter Four — What's in a name? _____ 46

A note on 'flexible working' _____ 52

True flexibility: Results orientated work _____ 54

We have ways of watching you work… _____ 57

Chapter Five — Applying for a homeworking job _____ 62

Recruitment tests and tasks _____ 63

Sample work and assignments _____ 65

The remote job interview _____ 66

    Practice with the tech first _____ 67
    Check your sound and light _____ 68
    Check your background _____ 70
    Secure your environment _____ 71
    Be on time _____ 72
    Dress for success _____ 73
    Be prepared _____ 73

Chapter Six — Sorting out your home office _____ 76

Are you sitting comfortably? _____ 77

Get up, stand up! _____ 82

Watch your eyes _____ 85

Engineering movement into your home office _____ 86

Chapter Seven: A note about technology _____ 90

Work first, tech second _____ 91

Staying up to date _____ 93

Conclusion: So now what? _____ 94

Acknowledgements _____ 96

About the author _____ 98

Introduction

As my 20th anniversary of working from home approached, I wanted to celebrate it in a meaningful way. What had started out as a practical solution to caring for a new-born had become, for me, a lifestyle choice. It had on reflection enabled me to create the career I wanted in the location I loved, and I wanted to share everything I'd learned along the way to help others do the same.

When I drilled down into the details though, 'everything I had learned' turned out to be, well — quite a lot.

Two decades is enough time to identify trends, experiment with ideas, work with different ideas about technology and tools, and also to make lots of mistakes. There was no book on the shelf (physical or digital) to tell me how to do it, so mistakes abounded, with all their learning experiences. Even when you try very hard not to make the same mistakes twice, there are still endless new ones to explore, believe me… And these lessons weren't just about the work and how to do it, they were about myself too — what I needed to be well, fulfilled, focused, and happy while doing it, meeting my emotional and physical health needs within a life based around working from home.

So, the concept of 'Healthy Happy Homeworking', a manual of biblical and epic proportions was born. And I sat down to write my tome which hoped would help everyone else learn from my mistakes, triumphs and hacks, enabling them to take the fast track to work from home success. With the technology and connectivity that I struggled with for years now so freely available, more and more people were exploring the possibilities that home-based working has to offer. Brilliant, I thought, couldn't be better timing.

And then, everything changed...

No one could have predicted the events of 2020, and the accelerated focus shift this brought, as globally we grappled with the Coronavirus pandemic — and worldwide, businesses and organisations who had never shown the slightest inclination toward distributed working had to make an overnight decision: Either we shut down completely, or, everyone grabs a laptop and gives this their best shot for now. We'll work it out as we go along.

That story is still being written. For me, it meant competition for time and attention of journalistic assignments talking about distance working collaboration technology, and delivering remote transition client work, which it became quickly evident, was not conducive to writing a lengthy 'everything I know about this subject' type of a book.

Also, conversations with the people I was doing my best to support helped me realise that that wasn't what was needed now anyway — so the project underwent a total rethink and redesign.

How to use this book series

I realised that if you're struggling to remain productive, solvent, and sane during forced home working, during a global pandemic on top of your personal circumstances, then you don't have a lot of time to read long books full of anecdotal learning experiences. There's no more browsing your e-reader on your daily commute for a start, because where and how our time was deployed has changed overnight. What you deserve, and what you need, are short, sharp and tightly-focused reference materials which give you the ideas, information and resources you need fast, right at the moment you need them. And you need community, and connection, with people in the same boat grappling with the same issues, each in their home-based isolated workplaces.

This is why Healthy Happy Homeworking was rapidly re-visioned as a book series instead of a potentially overwhelming "guide to everything homeworking". Not everyone needs support with the same issues, so the guides will be released in sequence and updated as often as feasible, to ensure their content remains a valuable reference and source of support for every emergency home-based worker, as well as those seeking to enjoy the benefits of remote working on a long-term proactive basis.

So, enjoy volume 1, "Out of the Office: Making The Transition To Working From Home", and look out for volume 2, which will be all about creating and maintaining healthy boundaries around working from home, coming soon.

The books will form part of a sequence with minimal coverage of the same territory; they are designed so that each one stands alone and can support you individually as needed.

Is the Healthy Happy Homeworking series for you?

This book is for anyone who finds themselves working at or from home — whether through choice or through circumstance, and whether employed or self-employed.

It's not a book about how to find home-based work specifically (though it will help you navigate the hiring and recruitment process), nor is it about how to do your job. I definitely can't help you with the latter, though here too, this book and others in the series will explore ways to transition what you do in the office or traditional workplace to activities or ways to add value which might work in a very different environment. They will also suggest ways to cope if you find that your manager is lacking confidence or experience in managing home-based teams. Successfully working from home means managing yourself, perhaps more than you are used to, and finding different ways to make your work visible to others, while at the same time possibly redefining relationships with colleagues and clients.

While I am writing this book in the year 2020 in response to very unusual circumstances, I am first and foremost an advocate for remote and flexible working forever, because I know it has done and continues to work for me over the long term — two decades-long. I was a very early adopter.

I appreciate that it might not be everyone's first choice, and indeed many reading this may have been forced into it with no advanced warning or planning, but I believe there are ways to make this choice work better for you, even when the circumstances are not ideal, or even if it's the last thing you wanted. While this has been my preferred way of working for many years now, I have also worked with a lot of people who are new to the practice, even resistant to it, and I genuinely consider that anyone can learn to make the best of it.

Working from home can be a great lifestyle choice whatever work you do, and it can help you find the right blend of personal and professional activities and relationships to support you in whatever you want to achieve.

Yes, that's a big promise for a small book, but stick with me.

First though, a few more words to really clarify what this book is and is not:

No "business in a box", or even in a book

"Be your own boss", "work-from-home freedom", "the work-from-home lifestyle…"

Advice and promises abound, from those who have 'opportunities' they'd like you to be a part of or who are trying hard to sell you some kind of dream, based on a business-in-a-box, or a product that is so compelling it simply sells itself… Or you don't have to do any selling at all, you simply just have to do 'data entry' or irritate your friends on social media or post spam comments, I am sure you know the kind of thing.

If that's what you're looking for, I am afraid you have the wrong book in your hands — but two seconds with Google or any social network will give you all the leads you could wish for.

Caveat emptor.

For the most part in this series I am going to assume you already have work to do, either as an employee or self-employed contractor, and you need or want to do that work from home for the time being — or if you are job-seeking you already have some professional or administrative skills and experience that people are willing to pay for in some capacity.

That work is likely to be something loosely coming under the heading of 'knowledge work' of some kind — that is, you're providing some expertise that probably involves the bashing of a keyboard to create or process something digital, with varying degrees of creativity.

What I will share in these books will apply regardless of your employer or industry, and I will encourage you to think about all the different kinds of work you do and how that might fit into your daily routine of working from home or elsewhere, in ways that might be new to you.

But I definitely won't be able to help you get-rich-quick I'm afraid… I will though, I hope, help you see the potential for richness in many aspects of life, that working in a more flexible way can support.

So let's get started.

Chapter One - Flipping expectations: from the exception to the new normality

Before we dive in too deeply to the mechanics of transitioning to working from home, I want to share some reflections about how doing so has changed so radically in light of recent events. If this feels a bit whimsical and anecdotal, feel free to skip ahead if you don't need this context — because already in some sense the 'old' style of looking at working from home seems dated and nostalgic in many ways. It does though still give us some valuable context and perspective.

Unexamined assumptions overturned

Throughout my long years of working from home, the very fact that it's what I do has often been a point of curiosity in conversation, with opinions falling into one of three broad categories.

The first is to assume you don't *really* work at all. Even when I ran a growing research company with a team spread across three countries, you could see the instant dismissal and sliding away of a glance at times, particularly if it emerged in the context of being introduced socially as part of a couple. It could quite literally be *The little woman works from home? Oh, that's nice… As I was saying….*

There's nothing much to say about this kind of conversation, or correspondent, except that thankfully there are usually more interesting people around to talk to.

Reaction category two was more wistful, and particularly common when I met other young mothers, back in the days when working from home was still distinctly unusual. Especially people early in their professional careers who were working long hours on top of a long commute to meet someone else's expectations of a graduate path up the career ladder, who often spent a ridiculous chunk of their income on professional care for children they got to spend little time with.

"Oh, you're so lucky!" They'd reply, when learning I worked from home. And that was even before I moved from the suburbs of London to Eastern Spain, simply because we had decided that was a better place for us to live and raise our girls. Yes, I knew, indeed I know I was and am 'lucky', in so many ways… So much of what I had in my life was fortuitous and made me feel rich in ways which were different from those on different kinds of city-based career trajectories.

But that luck, it was also down to choices my husband and I had made at various points throughout our lives, sometimes difficult choices, and the taking of calculated risks. And I worked bloody hard for my luck at times — frequently being made painfully aware that I had to prove myself above and beyond office-based associates and clients, simply to justify being good enough 'despite' working from wherever I was.

And when I asked if people whether, as they clearly liked the sound of the idea, they'd ever considered talking to their own boss about working from home, there was usually quite a surprised reaction: *Who me? Nobody in my firm works from home! That'd never work! My job can't be done that way! My manager would have a fit if I even suggested it!*

Even though in the UK the right to have flexible working considered by employers has been enshrined in law since 2014,[1] relatively few people I ever met had taken the idea seriously enough to ask or make a case for themselves.

I was always glad to support and mentor the exceptions and help people make the transition, even just to explore the possibilities that the Flexible Working Regulations introduced — which ranged from compressed hours to flexitime to full-time working from home.

But the gap between 'oh that sounds like a nice way to live and work' to actually taking steps to change your lifestyle is a vast one, and not something that everyone would consider. It's important for me to remember this, when thinking about how much working life has changed for so many people in recent months, and not by choice.

Ask to leave the office, to work from home? The sentence was always delivered with an air of incredulity. It was similar to the conversations we had again a few years later when we decided to emigrate. And I'm sure some of those 'who me?' reactors were really 'category three' people anyway, who were simply being polite.

Because the third type of reaction that I have heard over and over again goes along the lines of 'Oh, but *I could never do that!*'

I could never work from home — I'd never have the discipline, the motivation. I'd miss the buzz and the social life of the office, I'd miss that London vibe and getting coffee at the station or whatever it is commuters do, the drinks after work, and all of that.

And I get it, all those little elements which go together to build a lifestyle and routine, as well as a career path which may include being visible at events and locations which matter, along with a social life and sense of identity centred around an obvious professional status. While I made a conscious choice in my twenties to never, ever commute again even were a gun to be held to my head, I could see that some people thrive on that collective energy of rushing around at the same time of day as everyone else.

Of course, there are also highly competitive career environments where specific kinds of showing-up are critical to success. While 2020 has led to many activities and events being reimagined online, I completely understand that this isn't the same. The tech and gets better all the time, but for group social and networking things, no one would argue that it's the same as a face-to-face interaction yet.

I am way less tolerant of the 'I'd never have the self-discipline' type of responses, and prior to everyone finding out the truth about their capacity to work from home and what it actually entails for themselves this year, I'd occasionally pick this as a hill I was ready to die on when bored at a social occasion. Yes, there I'd go again, wading the hell in to unpick those throwaway remarks.

But seriously...?

Yes, this is how the conversation generally went.

You're honestly telling me you wouldn't have the motivation to get up in the morning and start work — how on earth do you manage at weekends then, do you just wallow in your duvet around the clock? How do you do your housework and chores without the looming presence of a manager to motivate you? How do you see through long-term projects like home renovations, or tedious routines like your tax administration, when there's no one there supervising you ...?

Oh, you mean you are a functioning adult and you just get on with stuff because it's your responsibility to do so? Well actually, that's how it goes when you work from home. Or indeed, when you work from the office too, because when you think about it your manager probably doesn't actually stand over your desk ensuring every keystroke serves a professional purpose and you're not goofing off on social media instead...

No, they hold you accountable by some kind of review process based on agreed performance indicators, and in most cases, they probably leave you alone to get on with it between times unless you request their input on something. In those between times, you may well goof off on social media, load up your Netflix queue or chat to your friends online — even stare blankly out of the window for a bit, despite the fact it's all in paid for work time, because that's how concentration works.

It's also how knowledge-work works. Unless you're providing a function like physically guarding an entrance or providing legal numbers or ratios of responsible adults in a safeguarding role or similar, *no one* is paying you to simply show up, even if a legacy of habit and employment law from the industrial era means that your compensation is structured around time vs. reward per hour or month or year.

So, that's how it goes when you work from home too. You work, you do other things, you do a bit more work until the work is all done, and it's time to do the other (non-work) things properly.

Anyway, that was my dinner party conversation starter for the past two decades. It wasn't as bad as it sounds, I exaggerate just a little, and I didn't always feel the need to rush into battle — but I do love the way we live and work and will always evangelise about it given half a chance. As such, it was inevitable that remote work and new ways to work became part of my regular beat as I transitioned into full-time writing and consulting.

For me, it meant so many good things, I truly felt sorry for anyone who rejected the idea out of hand and might never know the benefits it could bring their way. But I also had to learn to accept that most people were fine with that, sticking what they were used to — the same as most people wouldn't consider migrating to another country purely for lifestyle reasons. And that was fine, we had lots of other things in common to talk about instead.

Then suddenly, everything changed...

I remember watching the news early in 2020 and thinking wow, this new virus in China sounds a bit serious.

It got so bad that they had to lock down a whole city — imagine that, everyone confined to their homes except for emergency shopping trips, to live and work and do whatever they did within their own 4 walls under police constraint. Of course, I thought, that could only take place in a compliant and controlled population like China, where that kind of emergency law could be introduced overnight and people would actually obey it — you could never imagine it happening somewhere like Europe or the UK, right?

Then, there did seem to be sporadic outbreaks popping up in Italy, Spain, and elsewhere, how strange … Hmm. And suddenly a big tech conference in Barcelona was cancelled, as one brand after another pulled out, and then all the dominoes began tumbling, the world was crumbling. With growing disbelief, we all watched it unfold on the news broadcasts, on social media, coming closer and closer, and wondering when the powers that be were going to *do something* and sort it all out. Stop it happening here, where we lived.

The rest, as they say, is history. History which is still being written… At the time of this final edit, some of the Western world is starting to return to a very different work environment one step at a time, in staggered shifts and with 'social distance', and most people who can work from home are still being urged to do so most of the time, while other areas return to rolling local lockdowns not much different from those in the first wave. Whatever else the history books show when we look back on 2020, and that's going to need a volume of its own, one thing we can be certain of is that it was an inflexion point when work changed forever.

So this book follows a period of many weeks where working at home was the *only* option, due to legal lockdowns which prevented travelling to work for all but the essential people, those key workers we never knew we relied on so much. We don't yet have a viable and widely-available way to treat or prevent Covid-19, and as such people are taking whatever practical steps they can to minimise exposure.

All we know for certain is that work as we knew it is fundamentally altered now, and we're going to have to accommodate this very different portrait of what 'normal' looks and feels like as we move forward for the foreseeable future.

I suspect that working from home will be a big part of that ongoing normality for lots of people, either as their regular day-to-day or as part of work/employment that is something more flexible. Many may choose this, having learned how to make it work for them, or seen the potential of how it *could* definitely work anyway, perhaps if they had a bit more room and some dedicated space, or weren't trying to home-school their kids at the same time. And perhaps if they could work outside the home for at least some of the time — whether that was in a 'proper' office, or some other more local co-working space or alternative location.

Other people will of course be extremely keen to get back to the commute and the cubicles, and all that work and the office once meant to them before everything changed. Reconnecting with face-to-face networks, people and places will be top of the priority list, even if some of the ways people communicate and collaborate might have changed for good. Some people definitely thrive on close-up connection and shared experiences.

But maintaining any kind of 'social distance' (if there were ever such a poorly-named term to crash its way into the global lexicon) will simply never be possible. We cannot return to the previous 'normal' conditions, where vast numbers of people travel daily into city centres at fixed times to cram into expensive real-estate simultaneously. If you've ever been on a London Underground train before 9 am, this is surely blindingly obvious. Things cannot ever return to exactly the way they were — so some kind of flexibility will be needed in terms of timing, shifts, and the where and how we work. At least for the next few years while the risk remains… And long after that, if the psychological effects of a couple of months of lockdown are anything to judge by.

Also, as there already are emerging further outbreaks on a seasonal basis, we're going to have to anticipate further lockdowns and restrictions, on a local level which may remove choice all together again, just as people have had a taste of the 'new normality'.

And when that combines with the first-hand proof in the concept already demonstrated for many, a permanent change in the numbers of people working from home is surely inevitable. So the willingness and flexibility to embrace working from home will be a part of the future of work, whether we like it or not.

But *this* is not what I meant!

It's good to be in demand, I guess, even if it's for all the wrong reasons.

"You know all about this working-from-home stuff — help!" Chorused all the people I had annoyed at those dinner parties over the years.

And, yes, I do. Not only have I lived and breathed remote, flexible, and mostly home-based working for two decades, I also write and consult on the subject.

Honestly, it was a relief to feel useful, to be able to do *something* to help a world thrown into turmoil — I am not a nurse, or a delivery driver, or any of the myriad other key workers we depend on just to keep the world going, while we hunkered down at home. If I could help someone log on to their work network, secure a video conferencing call, find a way to build a project management system or collaborative workflow overnight, or simply help coordinate some electronic babysitting and an online Zumba class to preserve sanity, I was glad to do whatever I could.

Now, with the dust starting to settle — even though the air is not yet clear enough to show us what exactly the new normal will look like — I have time to write this book and the others in the series and talk to people about what the experience has taught them and how it's shaped their feelings about working from home.

It's clear that assumptions have been challenged and tested on all sides.

The companies who insisted it would never work for them — because of their unique culture or atmosphere or startup vibe — if they survived this crisis, it's because they found new flexibility over matters they had previously regarded as set in stone, and learned that they could endure, and even thrive, in a distributed setting.

From Silicon Valley to the City of London and everywhere in between, more and more large firms and organisations are now embedding home-based working into their long-term strategic planning. This is aligned with goals which go way beyond being only a response to the pandemic: they are realising and understanding gains in productivity, huge savings on real estate, and all the benefits of opening up recruitment to a wider — potentially global — catchment, as well as (yet) unresolved legal concerns over their potential liability for making office buildings into safe places to be as we learn how to live with the virus.

The managers at every level, who might have had years of experience but all gained within colocated offices (or at least a string of locations where everyone worked in one place) — who have had to quickly learn new ways of supporting people through the crisis while simultaneously holding them professionally accountable. They've learned tactics for making the work visible when the people are not, alongside, in many cases, completely redefining their own day-to-day activities.

Now they know it can be done, and done successfully — what will their response be if someone asks to make it a regular part of their workflow? What would they do differently, if designing a long-term solution to remote working, rather than lashing together an emergency response? And where will the managers themselves decide to work?

And finally, there's better acknowledgement of every knowledge worker whatever their role, and whether they manage other people or different resources or simply their own time and productivity. One way or another they have worked from home and lived to tell the tale.

But what tales, and what a time it has been... And it hasn't all been pretty.

Alongside helping people get their meetings and collaboration tools set up, I wanted to punctuate every call, every Slack message, by screaming (loudly but, somehow, also reassuringly) "but, it's not meant to be like this!

"This isn't what I meant when I said I loved working from home!"

It is NOT supposed to be this way.

I have seen friends working in tiny Spanish apartments, trying to supervise home-schooling for three under ten-year-olds, and finding out the hard way just how many people their broadband line was really in contention with. People working from shared space at a kitchen worktop, in homes designed for Mediterranean street life — where you don't need much accommodation for entertaining and relaxing at home, never mind working, because normal days are spent out of doors in social environments.

People who weren't big fans of smart technology so didn't have a range of devices at home for getting each family member online, instead having to share one laptop or try to have gear shipped to them just as all the suppliers ran out. People who have held down jobs and businesses in the most unbelievable circumstances, working ridiculous hours while alternating parenting and tech resources with partners scrambling to do the same. And doing all of this at a time of heightened fear and anxiety for their futures and the wellbeing of everyone they love.

I hope no-one ever tells these people they "can't be trusted" to get on with their work from home, or anywhere else they damn well please, because they have proved under excruciating and utterly unanticipated pressure that they can. Frequently they've done so with little support from managers who were flailing just as badly — not least because they've all been trying to get by with all the wrong hardware and software to support remote work in spaces never designed to be work environments.

And while some cannot wait for the all-clear to get back to the office even if they know it's going to be very different, others are fearful of exposure to the virus, of sending their kids back to school, or of punctuating the delicate equilibrium they have accomplished in the eternal search for life-work balance.

These are people who can see a future where they are not under legal lockdown, but don't have any wish to go back to business as usual either. Who have enjoyed reclaiming that commute time for themselves and their families, and wondering how they might want to use that time if they could truly spend it how they pleased. Who are thinking that perhaps home isn't the ideal place to work all the time — but maybe a local co-working centre would serve, or a coffee shop, or a flexible arrangement with some time in the office or some face-to-face meetings, but keeping their options open, because for the first time ever they've made the leap…

They've disassociated work from *where* they do it and made work into a **thing they do instead of a place they go to.**

That disassociation may have been incredibly painful and traumatic, and some may never recover from it — but for others, a whole new world has opened up, and is there to be discovered and enjoyed.

Chapter Two — The reluctant homeworker

A few words for you if you really hate this so far...

After many years writing for and working with teams and individuals about the transition to remote work, from time to time I have of course come across people who were less than enthusiastic about the whole idea.

Sometimes this was as a result of a corporate decision, such as the closure of a local office or a big restructuring. The offer of 'work from home or lose your job' is not the most attractive choice to consider, but it's not unheard of, and a variation of this is 'work from home, lose your job, or relocate your whole household to someplace you never wanted to live in.'

For most people, even those in single-person households, the choice to work from home — or at least to give it a try — is the most likely outcome, than to uproot to somewhere new, unless that really is a viable choice that might come with other benefits and opportunities. A couple of decades back it was a binary option, but for many, the chance to trial homeworking before considering relocation at least meant some potential to see how things went and maintain employment. Such a flexible attitude on behalf of the employee has often been welcome and helped to distinguish those who were willing to step up and help a business they were loyal to survive a rough patch.

I am sure that within the next few years a mass downsizing of office real estate is going to happen. Even though in the past this has historically been deployed as a cost-cutting move in times of stress, the future will bring change here at scales no one ever could have imagined.

But in some (albeit more limited) way we've been here before. I knew a number of businesses who took the step of closing an office following the 2008 financial crisis, simply because the renewal of a lease would have tipped them over a limit financially. They shifted to home-based working on what was agreed to be a temporary basis — let's get through this, then we'll find a new office and get 'back to normal'.

However, in my small survey sample, not one of those businesses ever did go back to renting a centralised office — a decade on, they're all still 100% remote. That doesn't mean their leadership team was deliberately deceptive about their future plans, simply that those plans changed.

Within the team I know best, a boutique PR firm, several senior people have since relocated a long way from London just because they realised they could, and collectively they solved the technical collaboration challenges that they faced to at the time (and this was a decade ago when the tools we take for granted were less available, harder to run, and more expensive overall).

They still work with lots of London-based clients who they visit whenever required, and meet in posh private clubs and business centres if not going to their client's offices. None of them has ever felt the lack of a central location — even those whose commute involves a long train ride from the West Country can cluster their meetings into one day a week and enjoy all their chosen lifestyle benefits the rest of the time. They also now work with clients further afield, and no one would dream of expecting them to open and maintain a branch office in each city within which they operate.

Alongside these benefits their hiring has become more diverse, allowing them to engage experienced senior consultants on a part-time basis, who would never consider returning to the commuter rat-race. They are able to reward their loyal and dedicated team competitively, not least as they're no longer pouring out a substantial overhead on a groovy rental in Shoreditch.

But I remember when they first took the decision to leave their Eastside hotspot there was considerable objection and regret from certain quarters, and even a minor amount of attrition — involving one mature administrator who went to work in someone else's office, and a junior executive who feared her career would not progress as fast or effectively if she wasn't visible around the city at events and venues. I wasn't able to contact that individual for comment, though her LinkedIn profile suggests a steady and successful career with a global PR brand, so I am sure she would regard herself as having made the right move for her in the moment. In the absence of a control group, who is to say — it was a courageous decision to leave a happy role for pastures new at a difficult economic time.

The main thing is, she had a choice, and she exercised it. Choice being the one thing that many people are lacking in 2020

So, if you're reading this far (thank you) and are still waiting for me to tell you that it's going to be OK, that working from home will be better for you despite the fact you had no option, then I'll do my best to persuade you of some of the upsides.

And if you're worried that it might turn out to be for longer than you are currently being told, you're probably right, it's highly likely to be. But if you **can** make homeworking work for you — and I will help you to do that as much as I possibly can through this book series — then you can enjoy multiple benefits at different levels:

Saved time

While home-based workers are finding their boundaries increasingly eroded by technology as much as any other executive, those boundaries are more under your control if you are within your own space (and we'll examine the sometimes sensitive issue of 'space' extensively in an upcoming book.)

Here are some interesting stats for you to consider;
According to Totaljobs:

The average London commute is 13 miles a day, 48 minutes long and costs £122 a month;
Londoners will commute over 141,000 miles in their lifetime;
Londoners will spend 363 days of their lives commuting.

(I am just taking London as an example here, feel free to check out the statistics for your own city).

Think of it along the lines of that dreadful metaphor of the boiling frog, who would hop straight out of a bubbling pan into one that isn't, but slowly and without noticing cooks in incrementally heating water. Commuting is death by a thousand late trains... Measured out in 48-minute chunks (or for some, much longer).

Put in a more positive way, imagine if your boss said to you, here — have a year-long sabbatical, to do whatever you like, here is a gift of those lost 363 days I owe you. Enjoy!

What would you do?

Write that bestseller (honestly, everyone has a book or two in them), get in shape (or train for a marathon), declutter and Feng shui your home, kick off that side hustle and try new recipes. Or just cuddle with your kids, have a lie-in, binge-watch Netflix... It doesn't matter, it's *your* time, and it always was.

When you no longer have to go out and catch a train, you can do what you like with it (though in a later book we'll need to have a talk about the potential implications of losing that walk to the station or the office on your physical wellbeing, because there's a reason the words 'healthy' and 'happy' are right next to each other in this series' title).

It's not just the commuting time you'll get back though. You'll probably find you save a great deal of time by multitasking in the broadest sense — getting your laundry done during the week, working around commitments which require you to be home but you're still able to get your work done (like waiting in for deliveries or supervising tradespeople). All sorts of things which would have meant taking a day off work to accomplish can be accommodated much more easily and flexibly into a home-working day, rather than a 15-minute dental appointment costing you a day's leave and productivity.

Saved money

Another way to look at those commuting stats above is to add up your own annual commute time — because no one is going to exactly match the average — and then multiply that by your hourly rate. Go on, do it (there's a calculator on your phone, but you knew that). Five days a week, multiplied by say forty-six weeks if we're generous with holidays... A nice sum, probably.

Again, imagine someone handing that money to you as a bonus every year instead — and yes, of course, we know it doesn't work like that in real life, it's similar to when people talk about how much money you'll save giving up smoking for example. But the truth is, there's nothing to stop you putting the money you save on your railcard (or indeed your tobacco) aside in a savings account and letting it pile up, is there?

There's more too, because I am sure I am not alone in spending money at a higher rate when leaving the house. Putting to one side any lockdown-exacerbated Amazon habits of which I may be guilty, I know that whenever I go to meet clients in their offices I end up haemorrhaging spending on coffees, magazines, cabs, and things like that, things which never come up when you're working from home, and can be tricky to expense and account for appropriately in many cases. Oh, look, there's a sale on at boutique I have to walk past!

Of course it's lovely to go out to a coffee shop or bar or restaurant with a friend, but that's out of choice — not as a consequence of getting from A to B. And I don't mean purely social costs. I mean the little trails of spending which seem to go with moving around, which add up unexpectedly, real but somehow hidden.

And last of all, the working-from-home wardrobe is very affordable, even if your role requires a degree of webcam-smart workwear from the waist up. Out of the camera's angle of pickup — which you should check carefully — anything goes, and in my case gets dictated by pure comfort (or future intention, as despite years of evidence of self-delusion I seem to have this idea that sitting working all day in gym clothes might make me more likely to do some exercise later).

Homeworking hair and make-up can also be decidedly low-maintenance. Once you realise that everyone looks pretty washed out on a webcam the pressure's off, and you can decide that future salon visits are about pampering and ego alone rather than maintaining any kind of appearances for their own sake.

Saved communities

Looking outside of personal benefits, or even how nice it is for members of your own household to have you around a bit more, there are much wider benefits of home working too.

For decades, economic development experts have seen the impact on villages and towns across the world of urban migration. As traditional industries and businesses decline in favour of global enterprises and centralised manufacture, local opportunities for employment and career development decline along with them, and younger generations vote with their feet.

This phenomenon has always existed of course, but the

magnitude and its impact are greater than ever in recent years. Smaller cities and towns can't compete with big ones to attract large employers which bring jobs and resources into areas where people already live, so the people move instead. This then drives up housing demand, often changing the character and demographics in the area as well as pricing out those who traditionally lived there, and sometimes making specific locations worryingly dependent on single large employers.

As the cost of living in those locations goes up, people have to move further out to find affordable accommodation and commute times (and costs) grow... It happens in isolated bubbles, often around specific industries or even single corporations. In San Francisco from 2013 to 2016 housing prices increased 80% for single-family homes and 60% for apartments and condos, and things are similar in London, Dublin, and other central locations.

Meanwhile, the smaller communities those young professionals grew up in find their local businesses and facilities fading away due to lack of demand, and the vicious cycle of lack of inward investment escalates. Places where once there were real senses of community, are ageing and dying along with their remaining residents.

Some locations have taken drastic measures, with some villages in Italy and Spain giving away village houses for token sums, to try and attract younger people and families to return. If schools, shops and leisure facilities also reinstall this might work, but people in these regenerating areas will still need work to do. So they had better put decent fibre broadband in while they're at it.

More creative is the approach taken by some US cities such as in Vermont and Oklahoma who focus on the benefits that remote workers can bring to these communities. If people bring their own work to the new location, then the town doesn't have to provide tax breaks to businesses to open branches there, and so they're giving it to the new residents instead!

It makes total sense — anyone working remotely for a large employer can now relocate to Tulsa or Burlington and receive financial incentives to do so, while enjoying affordable (compared to coastal hubs) high-quality housing, and a high standard of family living. They spend their wages in their new hometown, flowing value back into the local economy and fuelling hospitality, leisure and other sectors to develop around them and improve their quality of life.

These have been isolated schemes so far, and the Tulsa one is very locally and philanthropically driven, but given the current inflection point where so many huge employers are now introducing home working as a long-term strategy, who knows what societal shifts we will see develop? Why would you pay Silicon Valley rents, when Google says you don't even need to come to the office?

Some visionary companies like Zapier are even paying employees a bonus to move *out* of San Francisco. For the tech industry, it's an example of a complete about-face for everyone who remembers when Marissa Mayer, the chief executive of Yahoo, forced employees back into offices in 2013. "Some of the best decisions and insights come from hallway and cafeteria discussions, meeting new people and impromptu team meetings," a company memo explained then. Well, 2013 was a geological era ago in collaboration technology, so perhaps we just needed better and different ways to 'meet'.

Combining these trends with the close-up view of their costly small apartment walls and no access to outdoor space that many people endured during lockdown confinement in big cities at the height of the pandemic, it's easy to anticipate exciting changes on the horizon... People trading up their lifestyles and reframing their priorities in ways which can only be good for the broader picture of economic development and regeneration, and the overall well-being of everyone. (Well, unless of course, your job is renting office real estate in downtown hotspots).

A Saved Planet

Commuting doesn't only cost *you*, incidentally.

The impact on the environment, of millions of people migrating en-masse into city centres and back every day is hard to put a price on.

We got some glimpses of its true effects during the 2020 lockdowns, with air quality in city centres being measurably improved, and 11,000 air pollution-related deaths avoided in Europe during April 2020 alone, according to the Centre for Research on Energy and Clean Air.[1]

At the time of writing many people are predicting that we will never return to the era of long commutes, low-cost flights, frequent business travel, and all that fossil-fuel burning casual moving around that the global economy took for granted until so very recently.

Of course, it's easy to forget that homeworking also has environmental costs, and you might well notice some of these in your domestic fuel bills for example — so you will want to investigate things like tax breaks, employer expenses, alternative

[1] https://energyandcleanair.org/air-pollution-deaths-avoided-in-europe-as-coal-oil-plummet/

tariffs or better home insulation to offset these.

Other less obvious indirect costs involve the vast data centres which now power the cloud-based communications and storage the working world depends upon because it's easy to think of data itself as not really taking up any resources or space — but at scale, this doesn't apply.

Nevertheless, compared to the cost of travelling backwards and forwards to an office each day, while difficult to fully quantify, the broad opinion is that working from home is better for both the individual and the world as a whole when done well.

Saved making a choice..?

Look, I understand — if you have read all of this, heard it all before anyway, and *still* hate the idea of working from home… and can't do a damn thing about it, then I am sorry, truly I am.

It's not my intention to try and sell you on the idea that homeworking is a good thing if you believe that it is not, and for the rest of the book series I will be focusing on how to make it work for you, given that it's happening anyway.

But right now, I want to encourage you to look the reality in the eye though, however uncomfortable you might find it, because you need, somehow, to make peace with the fact that this is how it is.

Events in 2020 have caused so many changes and so much economic hardship the truth is that right now most people do not have any choice about remote working, and *may not ever again.*

Businesses are simply not going to take the risk — and the risk seems to largely be placed on them by governments around the world thus far — of saying 'everyone, come back into the office now', when they have no viable way (be that practical or economic) of keeping people safe once they get there, never mind while they're commuting there and back.

And while many large employers are saying home-based working is being extended 'until the end of the year at least', everything I have learned from working with remote teams is that things will **not** be going back to the way they were when that point finally arrives, the sands have shifted too much.

Not only has social, technological, and business practice had long enough through this period to become completely normalised around home working, employers also have had time to notice and measure productivity and hiring gains. And if, or more likely when, the end of the year arrives amid the usual seasonal flu outbreaks and with still no effective way to cure or prevent COVID-19, businesses are going to extend remote working again for at least another twelve months, not least because they're trying to manage a sick leave/absence policy involving a potentially lethal contagion and fourteen-day quarantine advice/requirements.

And there is a very real possibility that maybe another twelve months after that still nothing will have changed… Between the alarming rise of anti-vaccine rhetoric worldwide, reports of reinfection/limited time immunity, and a range of other unknown factors, there seems to be no clear endgame here.

During that year ahead, leases will come up for renewal. Leases on vast amounts of office space in expensive inner-city locations, that no-one can imagine ever being fully occupied again. Inevitably businesses, who have had to dig deep to invest in secure cloud-based technologies and portable hardware to ensure safe and compliant remote working, are going to cut costs in an obvious and permanent way — by letting go of huge proportions of that square footage in a heartbeat.

Perhaps they'll offer you flexible alternatives like a budget for a co-working space or a way to work in colocation with a smaller number of colleagues in an out-of-town setting, but the traditional 9 to 5 and those rammed commuter metros have gone, and they aren't coming back. And whatever the HR department says about this being a temporary measure, somewhere in a private video meeting your board of directors is already having these difficult conversations — trying to squeeze an information security budget uplift out of thin air on the brink of an epic economic downturn and looking at big cost lines to slash.

What can you do about it? Not a lot, other than to be <u>very</u> clear about your own needs for you to be productive, fulfilled and sane while working mostly from home. You can lobby/make choices for that, as it is the most likely working option in your life for the time being… Prioritise what you need for healthy happy homeworking.

And I further encourage you to make yourself:

- visible

- effective, and
- indispensable in this role…

Because whatever economic upheavals await in the future for your current employer — if you have one — chances are your subsequent role will be home-based, or, at least home-centred. So equipping yourself for that situation in emotional, technical, practical and productivity terms, is the best way you can future-proof your career.

Chapter Three — Employment or entrepreneurship?

There are two ways to access home-based work, which are:

— firstly to find a job where someone will pay you to do the work from home, or alternatively
— to create your own work through self-employment

(Come to think of it, these are your two main choices when it comes to finding work of any kind anyway).

The latter certainly used to predominate for remote roles, and it's what I am most used to in recent years — in fact, I wouldn't have it any other way now, I love it. Having done various employed 'job-jobs' over the years I long ago realised that in each of them there were bits I loved and bits I hated, activities which played to my strengths where I felt fulfilled and in flow, and other parts where the time dragged and stress built and my best would never be good enough.

When someone else designs your job description this is inevitable, because a job description is basically a bundle of tasks and areas of responsibility that someone has bundled together, sometimes more arbitrarily vs logically and based on what the organisation has a need for, as well as what activities traditionally associate together to create recognisable professional roles, for which the job title is a shortcut. For me and many others, there's nothing to beat creating a role 100% for yourself, which enables you to spend time in your zone of maximum joy and productivity.

But I also know that what I love most about self-employment includes factors which other people would find a real turn-off — the endless hustle, the relationship building, the variety (which often means uncertainty), and the lack of any guidance or professional support in the form of a management structure (like having someone to sit down with you and say, "really, a book series about home-based working, are you sure that's a good idea..?"). Not to mention the fact that you still have to do some of the stuff you don't see as your flow-state blissful superpower, like business administration and making sure you get paid, for example. Yes, eventually you can outsource a lot of this activity, but you remain 100% responsible for its being done.

Having fallen into full-time freelance writing not exactly

deliberately, it has been the most rewarding and fulfilling work I have ever done, and taken me to new places both literally and figuratively — *but* I also know people who have tried under similar circumstances and found it absolutely was not for them.

A lot of what we'll talk about in these books relates to self-knowledge and being honest with yourself about what you need and want, what inspires and motivates you to be fulfilled and productive and emotionally well — so kidding yourself along if you're in the wrong role runs absolutely counter to this (and I speak from experience on that front too).

So, the alternative to self-employment is to find a job where you can do all or part of it based at home, and that is, ironically, now easier than ever.

Remote jobs: Default or orientation?

When I started out in my first home-based role this was definitely not the case, but the weird experiment the world has embarked on in 2020 has certainly proved a couple of things beyond doubt:

- that a great many more jobs than anyone ever dreamed of can be performed by someone based out of their own home, and,
- that most people can, at a push, do their work with this kind of indirect supervision. Indeed, often doing so in far from ideal circumstances.

So if you're looking for a job but you want to work from

home, then I anticipate you'll see not only far more roles specifically advertised as 'remote option' or 'remote-friendly', but that there will be plenty of other opportunities too which don't mention it explicitly but are open to a conversation about how and where the work takes place. You just need to be ready to initiate that conversation.

From the employer's perspective, I know from my own experience here that through many years of hiring people for remote roles, the most difficult thing — until very recently — was always trying to identify people who'd make a success of that aspect if it were new to them. Even with the opening up the geographic constraints and being able to hire from anywhere, the experience of having worked remotely for any length of time was still so unusual as to be a 'desirable' factor at best, and usually meant taking a chance on someone who had never worked that way before.

Quite often too, their idea of what appealed about working from home was based on not even second-hand experience and might have included quite a rose-tinted idealised vision, which was not only a long way from the reality but also wasn't always a great fit with the character of the individual concerned. Or to put that more succinctly, in the early days I made some costly mistakes — costly on both sides — in hiring people who really were not suited to working from home at all.

Today the experience and evidence are much more abundant, and most knowledge workers will be able to talk candidly about their personal experience of working from home. They've had a chance to discover what did and didn't work well for them in those circumstances, and what they need in order to do it successfully — which opens up a world of new opportunities on both sides.

So if you are an employer and if someone is seeking to work

for you who would like to do so from home or in some other remote or flexible way, you would be advised to consider that idea carefully — because they probably know they work well this way and could be an asset to your business in these changed times.

However, you do need to consider carefully how you present the opportunity to them because what remote working or home working really means inside any organisation is different and can vary significantly.

Consider it from the applicant's point of view:

Decoding the remote job advertisement

If you're looking for a role where you can thrive as a home-based worker, I advise a fair bit of reading between the lines of any job advertisement to truly identify how the hirer really feels about remote working.

Of course, you need to do this anyway, when looking for a job. We all have our red-flag phrases and triggers based on painful experience and have learned to look out for code like 'willing to go the extra mile to keep customers happy' in case that means prepared to be treated like a doormat by ungrateful clients, or 'work hard play hard' signifying a 24-7 hustle culture you might find deeply off-putting.

It's important not to jump to conclusions as a lot of these phrases are liberally sprinkled around by HR execs without any real relationship to the role itself… "Meticulous attention to detail" — surely that's a good thing in most professional roles, but does it signify a really uptight and intolerant culture, or simply that they want the job done with integrity and care?

Who knows? My point is that the wording of the advertisement or even the job description itself is only a part of the story. You should shop around carefully and use review sites like Glassdoor to explore feedback on larger employers, Google potential employers at length and in-depth… By which I mean, get well past the first page results that the brand themselves might have more control over, to find unofficial insight such as social media sentiment and news.

However when it comes to remote-friendliness this is a relatively new area to unpick, and if your potential new employer is one of the many who have only just turned to mass remote working as a result of recent events, it's a lot more difficult to get feedback on what the experience has been like. Also, in fairness, it's much harder to judge — it might well be that they're doing their best to respond to fast-changing unimagined events in a reactive and clumsy way, and developing policy on the hoof, which is yet to be put fully to the test.

Again, look out for first-hand testimony, from present employees, perhaps those who have been through the transition with them: social media, personal blogs or articles, these can be very revealing.

But also, explore some of the phrases you might see in the ad itself for clues. 'This job *can* be done remotely' signifies something very different to 'this is a remote-first organisation'.

Remote-first roles

A truly remote-first organisation will be fully distributed operationally, even if some of its team members or even senior management share a location or building.

For example, all meetings will be conducted digitally, one participant per screen, wherever they are calling in from — as opposed to being held in a central conference room where the important people are gathered, and the remote participants stuck off on the wall somewhere. Or, if they use a legacy conference room, they may have invested in technology to enhance telepresence, such as a responsive central camera, which literally puts the remote participants at the heart of the meeting. Such devices can be voice-activated to orient the gaze of the remote people in the direction of the person who is speaking, providing a physical alternative to the way that some online meeting platforms expand the view of the active speaker.

Remote-first organisations may have no physical HQ at all, but many will make an effort to bring people together from time to time for a blend of social and business interactions, such as an annual gathering or retreat, as prevailing conditions permit. And they'll bring conversations and connection to one another digitally on a more regular basis, beyond the work itself.

Often these are the kind of things you can learn a lot from, both informally via social media and in company-generated official communications. You can discover where face-to-face encounters these tend to take place, if partners and families are typically included, do they make an effort to be truly inclusive with such events, even when it costs more to enable more far-flung colleagues to attend?

Consider what kind of diversity do you see within the organisation. If the ad says 'this work can be done from anywhere', and it's equally obvious that every member of the team is from the same nationality or ethnicity, then there's an glaring mismatch between their walk and their talk — so you need to consider these aspects against your personal objectives and fit.

How remote can you be?

Other roles will be advertised as remote but with constraints, such as 'must have permission to work within the USA'.

To me, constraints like this signify an unwillingness to truly embrace all that remote hiring has to offer because there are so many straightforward and legal ways to manage factors like employment taxes — such as engagement of a global employment agency, or the remote person creating a local limited company. Indeed this might well be code for 'must be part of US culture and immersed in that work ethic in order to fit in with our team' — which rarely gets written down so explicitly, even though it might be more honest.

When it comes to providing equality of opportunity, it would be far better in that case to state, if applicable, that up-to-date knowledge of US culture and working practices are required for the role, if that is the case, i.e. if it relates directly to the required experience to do the job. Then this attribute can be tested and explored during the application process and need not exclude someone who isn't presently a US resident for whatever reason. More often though I suspect this kind of arbitrary constraint is thrown in on the basis of an unexamined assumption that 'we want to hire more people who are sort-of similar to the rest of us' — which is precisely the sort of thinking which undermines any real commitment to diversity and inclusion.

Or it might be that the successful applicant will be expected to be available to work within specific hours and timezones, and a geographical range has been specified in the recruitment advertising because of that. Again, this is a case of taking a job-related issue — availability for meetings and conversations — and extending that into an irrelevant and unfair discriminatory factor, about where you have to be located. Why not simply state that you have to be available for team collaboration throughout normal business hours GMT, or whatever the actual condition is if it's purely work-related? Then a night-owl from New Zealand can apply for it on their merits, or a shift worker from Kansas, or whoever from wherever.

By effectively opening the opportunity up to more suitable candidates the company increases the chance of finding the best person for the role.

And that's a win for all parties involved.

Always on?

The issue of communication about availability requirements also tells you a lot about the collaboration culture of a business, and there is a world of difference between being available for something like a weekly review or daily standup meeting at a fixed time and time zone, and generally 'being available' throughout a given time period corresponding to a working day in a given location.

What this can instead help you understand more about is one of the most difficult things to get a sense of prior to joining a team, which is the way they work together and communicate.

Naturally you will glean some sense of this from the role itself, and the extent to which the tasks involved are likely to be interdependent with those of other people. If you're hired to work as part of an agile software development team you can expect to be in a continuous flow of communications with your colleagues at all times. They'll probably have tools and structures in place to facilitate that kind of 'working out loud' for paired and mob programming, where you collaborate on shared repositories and liaise closely all day. As such, working in the same time-zone — or at least at the same time — as your colleagues, might be essential.

Conversely if you're hired to write lengthy reports, you should be able to anticipate long periods of deep and uninterrupted work — and this isn't consistent with a requirement that you will be logged on to a collaboration or chat platform between the hours of x and y.

All of this brings us to the much more complicated discussion about how remote work is managed and supervised, which will be explored in detail in a later volume in this series. Although we'll take a look at it in book two about boundaries because you cannot get that kind of deep work done if you're expected to be engaged in constant online banter and communication all day.

What's your side of the deal?

A further clue as to the remote-readiness of your potential hirer is to look at their expectations of what you would potentially provide, to work for them at home.

Again, bear in mind that this might currently be a policy thrown together in a reactive way, and that standard models are few and far between anyway for lots of industries. But your prospective employer might require that you can offer any, or all, of the following:

- A private dedicated room or space for working from home
- A broadband connection with minimum upload and download speeds
- A desk and/or chair suitable for full-time use
- A printer and or shredder, if you'll be working with paper, and if you're handling anything confidential
- A minimum standard of Mac or PC on which a virtual desktop can be installed
- A reliable phone/voice connection

… And so on.

They might offer to provide:
- Expenses for your broadband
- Ergonomic desk/seating to a given standard
- Budget to kit out your own home office to your preference
- Budget for co-working or other shared local spaces
- A dedicated laptop/computer, or budget for your preference
- Suitable mobile devices
- Tech kit beyond that which strays into the realm of toys and entertainment…
- Budget for personal and professional development
- Centralised software licences

Obviously, some of these clearly cross over into the domain of 'perks' and are more common in competitive hiring markets like specialist software development. It's not so much what they provide (although this is important) versus what you do that will provide the clues, but more about the thinking behind it all that I encourage you to reflect on.

Have they considered your needs beyond the work itself, for comfort and wellbeing? Are they considering your context as an individual, who might work best using your preferred hardware and operating system, and who might enjoy the flexibility of not being at home 100% of the time?

Do they offer you choices, such as providing a budget for equipment rather than a centrally-purchased model? Do they want you to grow with them personally and professionally through the provision of a training budget, personal project time, or even time to volunteer and serve in your local community?

Recognising your ability to work from home successfully depends on the creation of boundaries, the support of others you might share space with, is important — alongside the fact that you do not do the work in a vacuum. This can tell you a lot about the culture, expectation and readiness of the homeworking-friendly organisation to work remotely. So be sure to tune your radar in carefully to the signals your remote employer is sending and read between the lines to try and get a clear idea of cultural fit.

For a start, what do they even mean by the phrase 'remote work'...?

Chapter Four— What's in a name?

I work remotely

I work from home

I work flexibly

I am office-optional

I work on a location-independent basis…

All of these terms get thrown around on a fairly indiscriminate basis, and sometimes HR people throw in other frameworks like "agile working" (which in this sense has nothing to do with agile software development), or another favourite "smart working" — all of which terminology tends to embrace in some way the big idea of not having everybody come together in one building from 9 to 5 every day.

While these concepts do have some broadly accepted distinctions they are often used interchangeably and confusingly, and with the exception of 'flexible' working (which usually means something a bit different, see below), there's a lot of overlap.

Remote working covers all of it, pretty much, meaning you will be working at a distance… Though for many entirely remote organisations without a central HQ this obviously begs the question "at a distance from *where*, exactly?" It generally accepted that it suggests that the location of the work isn't important, though whether it's truly location-independent enough to be done from a beach in Bali may not always be obvious — so if you see yourself as a potential digital nomad, you'll need to get clarity on expectations here.

For anyone new to homeworking as a result of the 2020 global health crisis, it is important to be clear that **remote working does NOT have to mean working from home.**

Homeworking is one small subset of the places from which most jobs can be done remotely — although of course, it's possible that this is a condition or constraint, for example, if you work involves highly confidential casework and phone conversations which cannot be done from a public location. In such cases, your provision of a suitable environment to meet this need might be contractual. Or if the work you're doing requires especially cumbersome equipment which will not fit in the average laptop bag, like your darkroom or your 3D printer for example, that naturally creates its own constraints.

Assuming your work can be done without either special set-ups or high levels of privacy, and assuming you're not subject to any kind of legal lockdown, a lot of roles which are hired for as 'work from home' can in fact be carried out from a range of locations. These can include dedicated co-working spaces, cafés and coffee-shops, as well as more ad-hoc spots like trains and airport lounges, or that Balinese beach, so it's worth bearing this optionality in mind.

Indeed for many, the whole idea of working from home is anathema or at the very least a non-preferred option, from a social isolation point of view. Some people absolutely thrive on the buzz of the office environment, in which case you could look at swapping your daily commute for a stroll to your nearest co-working centre — where you can chat to other remote workers who use the same place on a regular or intermittent basis, share a coffee machine, and often access low-cost meeting rooms and mailbox addresses. I believe such spaces are due to bring a huge renaissance to local high streets and town centres which have been in decline for years as commuters dashed past them to their early morning trains, and now have the potential to breathe new life into the communities where they actually live.

Or if you don't have a co-working option handy, many cafés and coffee-shops are very friendly to digital nomads coming and going — even to the point of offering free power supply connection as well as Wi-Fi, provided you have the decency to keep buying something to eat and drink every now and again. Recently some pubs in the UK have started offering packages of a socially-distanced table with power supply for a fixed batch of hours, including lunch and infinite hot drinks — an enterprising solution for the burdened hospitality industry, and a great idea for switching up your work environment. Some employers offer a specific expenses stipend to cover these costs, in recognition of the mood and productivity gains this represents, for people who need such an environment in which to be at their happiest. (Perhaps if you're really lucky they'll offer a gym membership too, to offset the inevitable cakes which tend to accompany the caffeine...)

Of course, it's not just about mood and mindset, it might simply be about the availability of space.

It's easy for me to forget after working from home for two decades, and as a result, having taken this need into account in every decision about accommodation, that many people, particularly in urban areas, have no suitable space in the home to suddenly install an office — not without intruding on other members of the household or normally shared areas anyway. So being able to discover third options which are outside the home, but not in the office, can open up a world of new possibilities.

For me, as a hermit-like introverted writer, it's always been about working from home. I have tried to commit to co-working and regular interaction with other humans during the working day, but I am clearly far too stuck in my ways, and I have ended up wasting co-working subscriptions and breaking resolutions to walk to attractive cafés because I have everything I need in the spare bedroom and so to me, it just doesn't make sense.

I even lived right next to a beach in Spain for three lovely years, and spent many happy hours there... But never with my laptop. Real life working from home is not the stock photo image that is often presented. Palm trees don't provide enough shade, and AppleCare does not extend to sand damage warranty.

What I do appreciate though is that I *can* work much more flexibly if I need to, and just because my optimal comfort level demands a big second monitor, old-school paper desk planner, and a stash of different coloured highlighter pens and sticky notes, all I *really* need is my laptop… Which can be taken with me on travels, and lets me truly work from anywhere, even on the move if required.

Occasionally I set myself a crazy challenge, like to work from a different coffee shop for at least an hour each day of a given week if I feel like I really need to give myself a creative push outside of the same four walls. It's always an interesting experiment, not least in terms of making me plan ahead for things I can easily do on one small screen without extra reference material.

I usually fizzle out on this though as I find my concentration isn't as good, and I always feel uncomfortable about taking up space and spreading my stuff around, as well as the etiquette/practicalities of what you're supposed to do about watching your laptop and things if you need the loo. Oddly enough I don't mind working from places like this from time to time if I'm travelling, but in my own town it feels, weirdly, like I am out of place and belong at home! Don't take any notice of my hang-ups though…remote working is a very individual experience, and that's really my whole point — you have the potential to make it exactly what works best of all for you and you alone.

In my work at Virtual Not Distant[2] we often prefer to use

---

[2] Virtual Not Distant Ltd, https://virtualnotdistant.com

the phrase '*office-optional*', to address the idea that the work itself does not dictate the place you do it — although a traditional office could indeed be one of those places, for some or all of the time.

And that office could be a hybrid environment — it may have people coming and going, doing a few days based in the office while they have other days at home, or people hot-desking and sharing meeting space flexibly. Such a hybrid team might also include some people who never or almost never come into the office, along with some who do all or most of their work there every day.

Other complex models have sprung up under names like agile or smart working and revolve around the intersection of the work itself as well as practicalities like desk and meeting space. So someone might work around 60% of the time from home but come into the office a couple of times per week for scheduled meetings, or specific activities.

Sometimes these schemes are introduced as much to support organisational goals for reduced real estate costs as to meet any expressed desire to work flexibly or remotely from the workforce — but with a bit of forethought and planning such set-ups can function smoothly, and I expect we'll see a lot more of them in future. Although the requirements of sterilising and making safe shared use spaces will create new challenges for organisations choosing this path, new applications of technology — from antimicrobial touchpads to voice control to occupancy sensors — are opening up new possibilities all the time.

A note on 'flexible working'

While the word 'flexible' can be broadly applied to most professional activities which you can do from different places, in employment terms flexible working as a concept most usually applies to timing — whether that's the flexibility to work full or part-time or something more complicated like flexitime arrangements.

In my experience, these are the kind of arrangements which can happen quite organically in small teams, where everyone can stay accountable to each other through shared tools and even line of sight on a practical level and enjoy a high degree of flexibility with minimal fuss. So when someone says "I've several evening meetings this week, so I'll be in late on Thursday", everyone knows that's fine because they're all on the same page. No-one's filling in timesheets or playing games, and there's a shared understanding which stops anyone taking advantage and exploiting their colleagues' hard work.

As organisations grow though this can easily start to unravel as it comes up against different expectations and mindsets, and people putting in different levels of effort as a consequence. This can lead to performance review issues, perhaps a requirement for time recording and accounting for hours worked, and possibly to growing levels of resentment. As a result, they can end up retrospectively implementing hugely complicated flexitime agreements and policies linked to the employment contract. This may be based on there being core hours of presence, with an expectation of flexing only between 7 and 10 am and then 4 and 8 pm, and employees not being allowed to accrue more than X number of hours of unspent time or carry forward more than Y hours at the end of the month... This doesn't sound very flexible to me.

I cannot begin to imagine the overhead of administering such a scheme, and I wouldn't be at all surprised if the sheer complexity creates big resistance to adopting it to start with... But, if it means some people get to fit their work into their lives more successfully as a result, then good for them.

It's funny how many assumptions are implicit in the idea of what a full-time job entails in the first place, the great difficulties involved in defining anything that diverges from it — that is the typical 9-5 office day which has its roots in the assembly lines and production systems of the industrial revolution, and around which the guiding principle of the level playing field always centre contractually — as though everybody's productivity and effectiveness per hour was the same. Surely work has changed, even if the minds haven't?

But as in everything else in life, legal and regulatory change is years behind socio-economic and technological change, so various attempts to solve this pragmatically have been made.

Other forms of flexible working within employment contracts can include -

- a pro-rata part-time job, with salary based on a share of the full-time equivalent
- compressed hours, a variant of flexitime which might involve working a full-time role over four longer days
- annualised hours, where you somehow measure exactly what hours you do over a whole year
- staggered hours or shifts, where you're doing work at different times of day to your colleagues

Under UK employment law there are many different approaches which can be taken, so it's worth exploring all the possibilities if you need to negotiate with an HR department.

Job-sharing is also another way to approach work which needs a continual, or business-hours-typical degree of presence — so that work is handed off mid-week to a colleague who covers another side of it for you.

This kind of flexibility was commonly on offer in the large higher education institution where I did my last ever 'proper' job, and it was seen as a bonus for parents, academics, and others who could not or preferred not to work the typical office hours. But I am sure it would have made far more sense to look at the role more holistically and decide first whether it actually required X hours a week to carry it out, and whether that truly necessitated presence in a specific building or not. So much time and resource seemed to get soaked up every week in handovers, which could often have been better managed by dividing the work more permanently across different responsibilities on a project basis, in roles where relatively little of the work itself needed things doing for them during each of the five-day working week.

True flexibility: Results orientated work

The best kind of flexibility involves the trust and structural accountability to perform the work you're hired for, where, how, and (within the constraints of deadlines) when, you best feel it needs to be done.

Work for which performance is measured by the outputs you deliver, and nothing else.

This is sadly, in employment terms, a rarity, probably because contractually it's a very grey area, and means treading a careful balance between the performance expectations and the time you expect it to take to get things done.

Of course in contract and freelance assignments, this is an absolutely normal way to work. If a client hires me to provide an article of a given length on a particular theme, perhaps with a suggestion or introduction to a couple of sources to interview, then we agree on a fixed cost and a deadline for the first draft to be submitted.

After that it's up to me to manage my time, pin down the interviewees, and produce the copy — and it doesn't matter to the client whether that takes me an hour or fifteen hours, their deliverable is the same and so is my fee. If I procrastinate, a source messes me about, I have a technical problem, personal issue, or I overcommit, then it's up to me to burn the midnight oil — or to try to renegotiate deadlines, while bearing the risk that that editor might never commission me again because I've proved unreliable. Conversely, if I have one of those glorious days when everything flows and the article seems to write itself, then I'm done and off for an early walk, or I get more time to work on personal creative projects.

For me and thousands of others this is the most natural way to work, and the most flexible and fluid. It allows me to focus when I feel at my most productive, and to fit in whatever personal plans or dates I want according to what the schedule allows. I tend to keep my mornings free for writing because that's when I do it best, whereas a friend who is a software tester can't really get started till after midnight — she *can* work during daylight hours but it will take her longer as she's less productive. In my case I can write very early in the morning if I accidentally find myself awake, but anything which counts as the night before is a terrible time for me to attempt to be creative about anything.

Obviously, this kind of flexibility in the freelance world brings with it all the hustle and uncertainty that many people dislike, so the holy grail in this context is to identify a **results-oriented work environment** (sometimes called a ROWE) that comes with a regular pay-cheque.

The ROWE framework, created by Jody Thompson and Cali Ressler in 2012, is a blueprint that many organisations have experimented with formally, and other managers have adopted more informally. At its heart, it simply means holding people accountable for outcomes and fulfilment of performance indicators, rather than the processes and activities used to deliver them.

It depends on huge amounts of trust and psychological safety, as well as explicit understanding of roles and accountabilities, and in the absence of these elements the framework can crash and burn fast. A classic example is if someone thinks they're pulling their weight and being a responsible team member but actually their manager or colleagues see things differently, simply because they're not measuring output or effort in the same way.

It's worth bearing in mind that in lots of professional and creative roles, a mutually satisfactory unspoken ROWE can evolve where trust is strong. When everyone works full time, brings total commitment to their work, performs at a high level, and doesn't feel a need to compete, there's no need for presenteeism or paranoia either… And this can apply equally well in a colocated or remote team.

We will return in more detail to this crucial issue of trust in other books in this series, because it affects so much about how we connect and collaborate and communicate in remote teams. But for now, I'll just emphasise looking out for this approach — and, sadly, also for its opposite which is paranoid micromanagement of the activities of the home-based worker.

We have ways of watching you work…

Tracking software, timesheets, clocking in and out, even keystroke monitoring… The kinds of policies which scream 'I don't trust you to do what you're hired for' or sometimes, 'I have no idea, as a manager, how to know what my remote team is doing — so here's a good way for me to deflect that anxiety'.

For me, this is the biggest red flag in the book.

Unfortunately with so many organisations and managers being forced to adapt overnight to supervising people they can't see, a consequence has been an explosion of tools which trade on that anxiety. These offer to track all sorts of aspects of the work itself, things which the manager probably wouldn't observe directly, even if they were sat in the same room.

I once hired a developer via an online platform to work on integrating a couple of apps, and we agreed on a fixed cost for the job. But he was used to working on lots of hourly-paid contracts and enabled the platform's own app to track his work, which took screenshots of his desktop every 10 minutes or something, and sent me copies of this while he was logged on and working.

Honestly, it was completely pointless — if the code on his screen meant anything to me then I probably wouldn't have needed to outsource the work in the first place. All that mattered to me was the final demo which showed me what he'd made it do, and that was the contractual milestone I needed to sign off on his payments. What if he'd had confidential stuff on his computer, content of his own or IP for other clients? I quickly stopped looking at the screenshots as they felt intrusive, as well as meaning nothing to me anyway, and not being good use of my own time.

Of course, many people find they are more productive if they feel a sense of accountability to others, and there's lots of evidence that people often perform at a higher level when they know someone is 'watching' or 'monitoring'. In general, we raise our game, and we respond to real-time feedback.

And here there are interesting parallels with the reopening of professional sports fixtures after the enforced confinement period, but with an absence of stadium crowd presence. Players report feeling less motivated and encouraged when there is no immediate reaction and feedback, no-one to put on a show for. You can also observe the very mixed success of live performances like standup comedy or panel/game shows, now being recorded and broadcast without that live audience feedback. It reminds me of delivering webinars a decade ago, when the software available usually meant presenting to your own slides in full-screen and having zero feedback until the end, unless someone texted you to advise that your internet connection had failed and your presentation had been frozen for the past 3 minutes...

Feedback is important. As a freelancer, I have often joined in different forms of accountability collaborations for networking or simply having someone to talk to about what I am working on. A formal mastermind group where you set your intention and then report back at the next meeting on what you have achieved can provide a powerful source of motivation.

It makes a huge difference that these things are voluntary, rather than imposed externally, and some of the tools on offer to supposedly track the effectiveness of homeworkers have the potential to be very counterproductive — if 'what gets measured gets managed' is a truism, then you can easily wind up with misaligned incentives and measuring the wrong thing. Going back to the example of my freelance app developer, if I had been paying him by the hour, I'd expect that hour to include a proportion of time checking his email or even social media — but I could easily end up paying him for *more* hours if he had to go to a different device to do that, because of the tracking app he was running on his work computer.

So you can see I viscerally dislike these kinds of applications, and all that they signify about trust and performance and accountability, or rather the lack of it. Other people, however, find them effective, reassuring and valuable in restoring some of the edges and expectations that being away from a traditional office may expose a lack of.

Most important, in terms of defining and seeking the kind of home working role which will suit you best, is to recognise what's most important, your 'must-haves' and what enables you to be happiest, healthiest and most productive.

Chapter Five — Applying for a homeworking job

If you've made your way through all of the above and found yourself a home-based role to apply for, then great. You've been competing in a potentially global marketplace at the application phase, and if the hirer knows what they are doing then they should not be wasting your time or theirs unless they are convinced of your ability to do the work effectively.

Now all you have to do is convince them that you're the best person to do it, out of all of those they have shortlisted for an interview. While that's potentially a larger field of candidates than in face-to-face interviewing — where that means bringing panels together physically and booking out rooms etc — compared with the volume of applicants it isn't likely to be a vast number, and you're already in a strong position.

Recruitment tests and tasks

Depending on the role, it's possible that your prospective employer will require you to undertake some kind of test, either something related to your ability to do the job, or to your personal qualities and aptitudes.

Try not to be put off by this, as the latter are always fascinating anyway, and most importantly remember that this is a two-way evaluation in progress, and if <u>you</u> discover that you and they are not a good fit psychologically, then the earlier you both learn this the better. If you think they're using arbitrary scales to filter out perfectly good candidates, then that's their loss and another way for you to learn about somewhere you really wouldn't want to work.

Above all, don't try to second-guess the desired response, just answer as instructed from your personal viewpoint, and you won't go too far wrong.

Again, you need to bear in mind that lots of HR staff and team managers have had to adapt and reframe their hiring skills overnight to evaluate candidates they never get to meet in person, and that can create anxieties and insecurities on their part. They're used to relying a lot on instinct and intuition honed over years, which is to say a lot of the body language and other non-verbal cues that interview candidates give off. So they could be looking for reassurance and ways to create confidence and trust in their own (virtual) impressions. Tests and evaluations are all a part of that. And the remote hiring process will continue to evolve, and specific tools are being created and tested and brought to market as I write these words.

Skills-based tests are arguably more relevant for some roles than others, but the sad fact is that some people do act deceptively when job seeking, in ways which range from exaggerating skills to outright fakery of qualifications and testimonials. So, if it's possible to directly test skills that are essential for the role, then it makes good sense for a hirer to do so.

Administering those tests online in a way that absolutely cannot be cheated in the moment might be challenging, but one way could be to time it — for example, email the test instructions and logins exactly one hour before the interview at which they will be required to talk through the work they just created.

I spoke recently to a recruitment agency owner who specialises in hiring specialist programmers for remote roles, who requires candidates to undertake a test coding exercise with a webcam on and live-streaming of their screen, along with the capture of ID documents on video next to their face, at a level of scrutiny akin to banking 'know your customer' standards — but he had been burned before by people turning up for jobs with his clients who it turned out were clearly *not* the author of their supposed test assignments. So, for the same reasons that most academic examinations and professional assessments have not robustly transitioned to online administration at scale yet, you can appreciate the need for caution.

Other parts of the testing procedure can cover more general skills, and with a bit of imagination you can probe a lot of the vital but intangible qualities you might need for particular roles, without requiring knowledge the candidate doesn't have. For example with a project administrator role, I once created a task where I presented the applicant with an inbox containing ten email messages and required them to prioritise them for attention, draft a response to each if required, and outline any follow-up action required.

This told me a great deal about their ability to make decisions and determine urgency (i.e. pick up on the one which signified an impending crisis, then the one which could mean a brilliant new opportunity, etc.) It told me whether they could read and write to the standards I expected (because you can never afford to assume even that an application letter is entirely the candidate's own work), and also that they could identify consequences and plan actions.

So if you find yourself on the receiving end of such a task, think about what it is they want and are trying to learn about you from it — what elements of the job description or person specification they are setting out to examine. And then apply yourself to the task with that in mind, to make it easy for them to see how you tick their boxes and for you to provide your best response.

Sample work and assignments

Sometimes an advert or application process will require a candidate to work independently on a particular assignment, to showcase their skills to the interviewer.

The ethics of this are always tricky. What is reasonable, in terms of you putting your time in? Who owns the finished work, whether or not the person gets hired? What does it tell you, the candidate, about the attitude of the hirer? I have seen ads requiring the preparation and submission of a detailed marketing strategy for a given product, before even progressing to interview — who is to say they even need to hire someone, if they get enough of these handed to them on a plate?

For creative roles, I have often seen the idea of 'test articles' and so on… Again, it's a tricky one, because if you don't have a portfolio of bylines to refer to then this gives you a chance to show what you can do — but do you get paid for the piece regardless, who owns the rights to it, and what if they want the article but not you?

Lots of hirers are very explicit about their need to test specific skills through carefully-chosen assignments, and pay for that work to be done. Once again this helps it become a two-way process, because the way that test assignment is briefed, managed, and evaluated will tell you a lot about what it'd be like to work there regularly.

Trust your instincts — there are legitimate jobs, recruiters and roles out there for you — and if something doesn't feel right then when you're in your own home you don't even have to get up to walk away.

The remote job interview

So let's assume you made it through all the hurdles so far and have a real live online interview invitation… Congratulations! The following suggestions can help you to prepare and make the most of this opportunity (and are also useful tips for any online meetings you may attend in future):

Remember that this interview will probably be recorded, which might feel strange at first, but is a GOOD thing — it means that the content of your responses may receive more attention than you can count on in an ephemeral conversation. More people can be involved in the decision about hiring you, and it's certainly less likely that any discriminatory questions or behaviour will occur.

Also, get used to it, a lot of online meetings are recorded in many organisations, for different purposes.

Practice with the tech first

You will most likely have been sent a link to an online meeting platform, which you may or may not be familiar with. While the meeting link itself probably won't go live until the appointed time, you can look at the front part of the URL and work out what platform it is that you're going to be using, then get some familiarity with it ahead of the interview itself.

A lot of meeting tools require you to download either a full app or a browser plugin, something which could make you a few minutes late for the call if you don't do it ahead of time. Think of it as the equivalent to checking the train times and connections before a physical interview, it's the same principle.

Install it, practice it, maybe look at a YouTube video on how the controls operate — especially if you've been asked to prepare a presentation or similar; to make a good impression you'll not only want great work to share but the ability to present it confidently and competently. So in that case make sure you know how to the access the screen-sharing function, and how to share *only* your presentation, not your entire desktop.

Check your sound and light

Again, this matters for every online meeting, but never more than when making the first impression.

Make sure you use a decent microphone, so they can hear you and headphones so you can hear them. A ten euro USB headset with mic from any retailer is fine, or at a push, the headphones which came with your smartphone probably have a hands-free mic in them. Practice with them and make sure you select this device for use in the call, as your browser or application might default to using the probably pretty-average speakers and mic built into your laptop instead of the one you have carefully chosen and connected.

Remember that we're all good at tuning out our own background noise — which is just as well, as we often can't do anything about it. Have a listen though just in case there are things you can fix and be aware that the mic will pick up sounds indiscriminately and amplify them, like your shuffling papers, or your clunky jewellery — so avoid noise-making actions or objects wherever you can.

Your computer and your phone make noises too… So turn off your notifications and log out of anything likely to go bing or beep throughout the meeting. This saves your power, bandwidth, and concentration too, for your interview.

When it comes to lighting, make sure they can see you properly. A light source behind the webcam, i.e. facing you, fixes that. Natural light from a window is best if you have that opportunity. Not so bright that you're squinting, or that interferes with your seeing the other parties clearly on screen, complete with all their body language and non-verbal feedback throughout.

You-tubers and other 'influencers' often use white ring-lights, which cast a diffuse and clear bright light on your face, from behind the screen. But be careful if you're a specs wearer like me, as these can make for weird and distracting reflections in your lenses. One idea to try is using a light source bounced off a wall, so if you have a bright light in front of you maybe turn it away from you onto a light surface instead — this reduces hard shadows and glare.

No, it shouldn't matter, but you want the interviewers paying attention to what you've got to say, not those strange alien robot eyes. So practice ahead of time with your setup and tweak until you're optimised.

The webcam which is built into your computer is probably good enough, and if your budget for enhancement is limited then I'd spend it on optimising the audio, where tolerance is much lower for poor quality. That said, an upgraded camera will surely be a useful investment if you can stretch to it, and one time I would definitely recommend it is if you have one of those laptops, rare these days, with a webcam built-in low down near the keyboard rather than at the top of the screen. Giving the interviewer a nice clear view up your nose will doubtless make an impression, but not the one you meant. If you cannot beg, buy, or borrow an external webcam, then practice with your laptop on a pile of books or similar, to bring the camera lens up closer to your eye level.

Check your background

When you're on the call you will probably see yourself in a tiny little thumbnail somewhere in the meeting app, but you have no idea what kind of device the other parties are viewing you on — so imagine they're using an 8000-pixel high-definition professional conference room screen, and think about what they'd notice. What's behind you right now?

This has become such a curious issue in the age of 'coronamedia', where every news interview now takes place down the line from the guest's home-office, and professional staging of impressive bookcases or gorgeous interiors seem to be mandatory. The more esoteric and intellectual the book selection the better, or so you'd think… But don't distract your interviewers too much, with your eclectic library choices!

Alternatively, you can cheat and use a background image photo of course, though the interviewer may then wonder why.

These can also get weirdly distorting if you move or wave your arms around when you talk making bits of you disappear or change colour; they are also very demanding on processing power which can cause more mature laptops to spin up their cooling fans and add hiss when you least want it — see earlier note regarding noisy distractions.

You don't need to get too obsessed or overthink it but try to go for a businesslike image with nothing inappropriate in the background, or simply keep it blank and neutral. I have had candidates show up to interviews clearly sitting on their bed, and once with laundry hanging up to dry behind them, it is, in all honesty, difficult to put that completely out of your mind when choosing whether to select someone for a job. You cannot help but wonder how they would show up when talking to clients on your behalf when you can quite literally see their underwear flapping away behind their head.

I like to think I am a non-judgemental person however intrigued I am at these glimpses that video-calling offers us into someone's life, as we all have different homes and resources at our disposal… But wherever you live and however you share your space, a little forethought can help you make the best impression.

Secure your environment

This means banishing kids, pets, neighbours, tradespeople, etc, from the room, and if in any doubt also banishing them from your internet connection for the duration of the call. Yes, if you're hired then a new employer may be happy to pay to upgrade your line, but only if you make a better impression on them at interview than any other candidate — so why allow any factor to undermine that, especially when you can fix it upfront? Doing so shows respect and consideration for the importance of this call. And it goes without saying you should be on the 'best' internet connection you have at your disposal, whatever that looks like to you — consider hardwiring, negotiation with those who share it over streaming or gaming, and having a plan B in the form of a hotspot or mobile phone.

Similarly, don't take chances on your environment being somewhere NOT your home office. Fix an appointment time when you can take the call there, not in your car or on a walk or somewhere any external factors like noise or signal loss could impact on the impression you are going to make. This is a strange trend that has infiltrated online meetings now that the major platforms have good mobile apps, but the quality is never the same — your best camera is on your laptop or desktop device, and it keeps still too. Please do the same yourself — keep still that is, by being sat down. I have interviewed people who thought it would make a cool impression to be strolling down the road, but it just made me feel seasick.

Have a glass of water on hand and out of shot, just in case you cough or something, but I'd avoid touching it otherwise. People sometimes wonder what to do with their hands during interviews or meetings when they're a bit nervous — the good news, in this case, is that yours don't have to be on view at all for a video call, you can sit on them. Or wriggle and wring them privately out of the camera line if you want (though do use them to gesture for emphasis as you would naturally).

Be on time

Your interviewer may be conducting a lot of calls back to

back, and honestly, you have no excuses related to traffic or finding the place for not being on time.

For any online call there is zero excuse for not being punctual. There's no point being early you probably won't even be able to access the meeting room, so just be dead on time, instead unless they say they like you to be logged on and in a virtual waiting room five minutes early (in which case 'five minutes to' is your new exact deadline.). Think of this as your first opportunity to demonstrate your attention to detail and ability to accurately follow instructions.

Dress for success

Just as you would in any job interview. At the very least, from the waist up. Wear whatever you would if the interview were face-to-face in their office. You'll look good and will feel more confident too. Check your teeth for spinach or similar (*before* the call!), and consider how you are lit (see above). If you feel more confident with make-up on, wear it, if not don't — but be smart, tidy and have brushed your hair.

I have a friend who always wears a particular perfume when taking client calls online. Why? Because it's part of her personal grooming and feeling professional. So if that helps you too, go for it.

Block colours for clothes work well for all genders, something non-distracting, as does keeping things simple and professional. Fine stripes and patterns can behave oddly on webcams of different resolutions, and while giving an interviewer a seizure will certainly make an impression, it's not the one you want. Again you can see lots of examples of this in online TV interviews, which would once have happened in a studio and been vetoed by a wardrobe department. Dangly earrings are a bad mix with headphones or mics, you don't want any sources of noise competing with the amazing things you're going to be saying. There are also some great online videos to help you be Zoom (or whatever system) ready.

Be prepared

Again, just as you would for your face-to-face interview. But it's so much easier online, to have your list of questions for the interviewer to hand, or points from your CV you want to be sure to mention… It's great for presentation notes too. You can put them on a tablet, post-it note, or second screen, in a way you'd never dream of doing so blatantly in a face-to-face meeting. Just put your notes as close to your webcam as possible, so that you're not shifting your eyes too far away to glance at them naturally.

After that, my best advice is to behave exactly as you would in any interview for any job you really want — and good luck!

Chapter Six — Sorting out your home office

Once you've secured your home-based/remote job, you'll need to find somewhere at home to do the work. It's probably a good idea to think about this ahead of time.

In Book Two we will look at the issues of carving out suitable space for your homeworking in a shared household or living space, and how to put in place effective boundaries to protect your work and sanity as well as manage the natural expectations of others in varying circumstances. These boundaries go way beyond the physical space which we will look at here because boundaries operate on many different levels — which is just as well if the physical space is in any way less than ideal.

For now, let's focus on the specifics of your work situation itself, bringing it down to the smallest possible space you need to get control over, and that is the way you sit and do your work each day. Start here, and work outwards, to the practical, emotional, and metaphysical boundaries!

Are you sitting comfortably?

That's an excellent place to begin because you can't focus on your work if you're in physical discomfort. Of course perhaps your work is compelling and interesting enough to capture your complete attention when you're not quite sat correctly, but in that case, you are going to have big uncomfortable problems later on, either in a few hours or a few decades, depending on the nature of the issue.

Indeed, if you're planning a new home office, or forced to carve out a workspace in a home never designed for that purpose, the place you sit and work is critical. While NOT sitting for too long matters as well (see below), let's start by getting this bit of your workspace right because it affects so many things — from your mood, to your productivity, to your long term well-being.

If you were in an office, it would be your employers' responsibility to design and provide a suitably ergonomic workstation, for you to be comfortable and productive.

It's worth remembering though that under UK and other laws, it would be down to you to actually use that equipment safely and correctly, once you'd be shown how to do so. The most expensive and perfect workstation or desk wouldn't protect your lumbar health if you slouch or slump or simply have it adjusted incorrectly for your height. Nope, I don't ever recall receiving training on how to use a chair back in the day when I worked in other people's offices either but nevertheless health and safety at work has always been a responsibility shared between the employer, providing an environment, and the employee, making use of it sensibly. And the benefits of that are shared too: you're happy and you don't hurt in the short and long term, and your employer enjoys your greater happiness and productivity, and at the same time doesn't get sued or have to pay you for time off recuperating from a work-related injury.

When you're working from home you will need, in this and many other things, to take greater responsibility for yourself — at the very least speaking up if something isn't right. Your employer won't know you don't have an appropriate chair to sit and work in for hours and hours if you don't tell them. But once you do speak up it's on record, and they can help you do something about it. Of course if you're self-employed then it's over to you, but if your work requires sitting at a desk for prolonged periods then a purpose-built office chair will always be a deductible business expense.

And this is important, because neither a typical dining room nor kitchen chair, nor an armchair or sofa, is likely to provide you with the alignment and posture you need to minimise strain on your body while working at a desk. In fact, unless you have chosen furniture specifically for working or studying at home, it's highly likely that you don't have anything particularly suitable, as it involves a way of sitting that's completely different from when you are relaxed and at leisure.

Oh, and while we're on the subject, the word 'laptop' is distinctly misleading. Your lap is the last place you should do any prolonged work, it puts your head and neck in completely the wrong position and will only store up problems for the future. I remember an osteopath saying to my mother how much he enjoyed walking suburban streets in the evenings and seeing the glow of laptops and mobile screens from the coffee tables and sofas as he walked by… Thinking about all the lovely future business potential they represented, from those people hunched with their necks at strange and unnatural angles.

What you're aiming for is a neutral position with a relaxed posture, where you don't have excessive reaching or award angles to contend with. This is one very sound reason that it's really good to learn to use your touchpad and keyboard controls incidentally, rather than relying on a mouse, which makes you move your whole arm rigidly.

You want to be sitting with hands, wrists, and forearms, inline, and approximately parallel to the floor. Your head should be level and facing forward, with no twisting going on, in other words, inline with your body. This sounds really obvious, but I have seen people working on coffee tables which are offset at strange angles, that put a small but continuous strain on so many different joints at the same time, and I've been guilty myself too. All I can say is that you can get away with this stuff in your 20s, but in your 40s and beyond? Forget it, you're in body protection mode. Your feet should be level on the ground, or if you're a shorty like me, then a footrest can help.

Looking at your monitor shouldn't require straining or squinting, and your eye level should be roughly in line with the top of it (this is also good for video calling too, as your camera is probably located here). It should be directly ahead of you, though if like me you like to use more than one monitor then, of course, there's going to be some degree of offset and moving your head going on.

Because people come in all shapes and sizes, to achieve these alignments and positions, good chairs — and sometimes even desks — tend to be highly adjustable. Have a fiddle around, if something's not working, you're not comfortable, tweak the settings and see if you can make things better. There'll probably be a manual somewhere, even for that chair (Google it).

The perfect office chair needn't cost the earth, though it can do if you want to splurge. The Herman Miller Aeron is widely regarded as the market leader, and is infinitely adjustable to suit every possible body and posture type, responds to your movement, and is very lightweight. It looks cool too, but as it costs over a thousand euros I have always managed without one, and so can't speak from personal experience. At the other end of the budget scale, IKEA and Amazon and the like provide perfectly good models for less than a tenth of that cost, and with the former you get to go and sit on them too and swivel around a bit — preferences for angles, armrests and things like that being highly individual in any case.

You'll also find every price point in between, and if you can, I strongly recommend going to a showroom and sitting around in one for a while, exploring the adjustments, and seeing what you think, how it feels. Do bear in mind the finish of the fabric, that you'll be sat on for hopefully a good many years to come, and the climate in which you'll use it. Taking a tip from the Aeron in a different price range, I have a chair with a mesh seat and seat back, because I work in a hot country where ventilation makes a big difference in summer, and I would not want to be sat on leather or plastic for any length of time.

Another thing to consider is reducing repetitive movement, which can lead to painful RSI. Even the most perfectly ergonomic workstation can involve repeatedly reaching for the same thing over and over for example, which could cause an overuse injury. So it's essential to mix things up and change your activities, change your posture, and look for ways to automate or abstract away repetitive movements. Options could include using a hands-free phone or a headset, if you make calls all day, or shifting the alignment of a reference screen or document holder.

Once again your employer should provide or assist with this if you are doing customer service work or similar from home. Your comfort directly impacts on your productivity and being able to avoid repeating movements drives efficiency. It's well worth investing in quality that lasts, for example, a headset that is designed for all-day use, which is lightweight and comfortable, so when a call comes in it's already on your head. Hands-free via Bluetooth or DECT means you can move around freely, and that energy will infuse your calls and conversation (but remember these things need charging regularly, and a USB back-up is a smart thing to have).

Get up, stand up!

Now we've sorted out the perfect desk chair, it's time to remember that sitting is terribly bad for us after all, and we urgently need to do less of it.

Indeed, a couple of years ago there seemed to be a lot of research headlines screaming along the lines of 'sitting is the new smoking', decrying the classic knowledge worker posture as taking years from your life even when you were sitting completely ergonomically. From compromised posture to metabolic disorders, it seemed that sitting at a desk was killing us in unexpected ways, and the last thing we should all be doing-bad news for a lot of us whose jobs involve pounding keyboards.

Oddly enough, many of the problems highlighted by those reports had lots in common with those of a century earlier, when campaigners were fighting for assembly line workers to be able to *sit down* at their workstations, to alleviate the pain and repetitive strain injuries they were left with after a day's work. And actually, if you try to use a standing desk for hours at a time suddenly, you'll quickly learn how they must have felt. So — as so often when you dig around behind the headlines — the truth is a bit more nuanced, than 'sitting is death'.

But it's scarcely more complicated, and there's a clue in the mention of RSI above — we are *not* meant to either repeat small movements *or* to stay in one place for any length of time. Our bodies are optimised to move around — when you think about it, this was bred into us by evolution for thousands of years of hunting and gathering and responding to our environment by doing physical things.

So it's just the same in the office, wherever it is, you need to get up and move around.

Standing desks are great — for a while. What matters more is mixing it up and moving. It's a complicated idea to align with the advice above, to get your workstation optimised so ergonomically that you're utterly comfortable for hours at a time and can get into the flow of creative work without noticing you haven't budged an inch for hours. Still, the two aspects are intrinsically linked, and together support the whole.

The trick is to get a bit of motion into your habits, into your daily routine. It's counterintuitive when you're trying to be productive and get work done to think about breaking it up and moving around, and most workplaces don't provide for this (unless you work at some groovy tech startup with beanbags and slides). But when you have control over your environment as you do at home compared, say, with someone else's office, there may be more ideas you can consider than you first think.

Sit-stand desks which hydraulically lift up and down are fabulous, and they cost so much that you are likely to be seriously motivated to use it if you buy one, at least at first. Cheaper alternatives are desk risers which sit on your desk and just raise your keyboard/laptop up and down, though in use these can be quite awkward, depending on how much desktop "stuff" your comfort level dictates. They can also pop up and down a little unpredictably, and you also have to be careful about the position of cups of coffee while things are in motion, I think that for me the real problem is that I am not a tidy desk person.

I have a friend who has created a standing desk from an old bookcase, so she can get up and work in a different position from time to time. She also uses this for webinars and podcasting, making the most of the extra energy the standing posture provides her with, as well as breaking up her working day.

Nowadays, to my shame, my desk riser is relegated to the garden shed, though I do have a good investment chair drawn up to my cheap IKEA desk. I try to take a pragmatic approach and move around physically as much as I can remember to do. I have my smartwatch buzz my wrist once an hour, and if I am taking an audio-only call, I try to do it on my phone while walking around the house and garden, or further afield when not restricted.

I also find that if you let some of your domestic life blend into your working day, it builds in a bit of movement — pop out for groceries, sort laundry, pull out some weeds. Look at the sky, or at the very least out of the window for a few minutes several times a day, while taking a few deep and mindful breaths, especially if you just had a challenging conversation or period of intense concentration. This relaxes your eye muscles, they were never designed for focusing at a short fixed distance for hours on end, and can get the most difficult clients and situations into a new perspective.

It's good for your thinking as well as for your posture. Those primal ancestors kept their brains in tune by scanning the horizon and reacting to change; you can do the same. It increases blood flow to your heart and brain and helps you stay mentally sharper and more creative. Walking is a great form of exercise, and we're genetically designed to do it for many miles every day.

Watch your eyes

All the horizon scanning in the world won't stop your eyes deteriorating faster than they would by age alone if you spend a lot of time in front of a screen. In the UK you can claim certain optician costs against tax whether employed or self-employed, and having the right prescription eyewear if you need it definitely makes a big difference — so get that annual test, or whatever frequency your optometrist recommends. If you are wearing spectacles with all or any of the lenses configured for close up work, give some thought to the optimal focal distance from your screen, which will depend on your desk and seating configuration.

Lighting and glare too can be problematic and create continual eye strain. Again in a centralised office, this is someone else's problem, but at home it's yours, and if you're working in a spare bedroom or corner of the lounge then the odds of the lighting being optimal for screen-based working are long. The good news is, it's your home, so you can make changes. You don't need to go for corporate neon strip lighting, but you do need to give it some thought and be ready to experiment.

Be aware of how the light hits your screen and bounces back into your eyes. Too much light can be just as bad as not enough, and if you're trying to follow advice about facing a window for video conferencing then make sure it's not casting your own screen view into darkness you have to squint at. Many screens and laptops have useful eye-save modes and adjustments you can make, even to reflect the ambient light associated with the time of day outside, so get to know what yours can offer and set it to work for you.

Above all, if you cannot limit your work-bound screen-staring hours, then do what you can about your leisure time. If you are busy and stressed at work, and also stuck in the house for longer than you'd choose, it is far too easy for the end of work to mean simply swapping one screen out for another of a different size.

It's well worth trying to mix things up and do something different and give your eyes and brain a rest — try something different, for example, you can catch up with podcasts or audiobooks, or listening to music while strolling out of doors.

Engineering movement into your home office

We'll explore the benefits of exercise to your health and productivity later on in this book series. Still, for now, just remember that shifting things around can make you happier, fitter and more effective at whatever work you're doing. So when you are planning your work from home environment bear that in mind, and if necessary, take account of it in terms of the motivations and rewards you build in for yourself to your routines.

Yes, you need to play tricks on your future self or decide

about things in advance for when your willpower and motivation may be less robust, it's just like deciding not to have biscuits and cake in the house because you want to lose some weight. Decision fatigue is a real thing, so if you can, decide once in advance for more efficiency on aspects where you have that option.

I recently saw a deal for one of those cute little capsule coffee makers for next to nothing, and my first thought was, I really want one of those for my office — my own coffee machine! But after a bit of reflection, I realised that not only was I already tempted to drink far more strong Spanish coffee than was honestly good for me, at least when I did so currently it meant a stroll down to the kitchen each time I wanted one, often followed by a quick break in the garden.

The mini-fridge idea went much the same way too…

So if you can, have the fridge, and also the bathroom, on a different floor. If you use the printer a lot, set it across the room from you. Make yourself work for it, especially if it's a treat (more effective that suggestion for a refreshing beverage than picking up a paper document, obviously, but you get the idea.)

Do you need to meet up with someone? How about a walking meeting:

As well as being good exercise, there's something very powerful about the creative and collaborative process which comes from combining movement with facing forward together in the same direction, it's non-adversarial and levelling, and I enjoy doing this. You can always stop for refreshment afterwards, but if you're both typically desk-bound, then you could always suggest a stroll to start things off.

Some people go further to build in opportunities for movement and calorie burning into their offices, such as sitting on an inflatable exercise ball, which makes you continually use your core muscles to micro-adjust your position. I have never tried this, and not sure how it would work with the ergonomic desk-height principles, but it might work for *you*, so don't rule it out.

You can even buy desks with built-in treadmills or exercise bikes, which some people swear by... For me that feels too gimmicky, as well as being too expensive for an experiment. I would never try to lash up some home-made MacGyver version of this, you might get away with it for a standing desk, but anything with moving parts would feel far too risky to put a mission-critical laptop on.

I think too, for me, I don't ever want to work so hard that I really couldn't squeeze in a quick walk on most days — there's something kind of martyrish about the idea that you're so busy you genuinely have to multitask to get your exercise done in this way. Both walking and cycling bring their own pleasures, even if you do them on a static machine. I think I'd find it distracting anyway, to have to do things with my legs in a coordinated way while also thinking and typing (in fact knowing me I'd probably trip up and land flat on my face and/or keyboard). I will have more to say on multitasking in later volumes. So, I cannot speak to experience when it comes to these machines, but I would love to hear from readers who can comment from a more informed perspective.

Lots of little hacks to build regular movement into your working day are a lot simpler and cost-effective, e.g. drink lots of water, so you have to get up to go to the bathroom plenty of times is one of the easiest!

There are many ways to plan your space to include little tiny incentives and triggers to get flexibility into your day, even in the smallest of spaces. And these are the things which will make your home office space more comfortable and productive for you when you are in it.

Chapter Seven: A note about technology

Working from home means dealing with technology a lot of the time, both to connect and communicate with the outside world and to actually do the work in most cases. I love communications tech and write about it a lot, but you will find I try very hard *not* to mention specific tools and apps within these pages, and there are two reasons for that.

The first is simply pragmatic — it moves too fast.

This year alone has seen an explosion of investment and development in the tools we use to connect and communicate, all with unique attributes and features trying to address specific pain points for users. This is good news for me as a tech journalist and good news for all of us in the remote work space.

Recent months have seen not only a proliferation of new brands but also rapid updates and improvements in many old favourites, making them more accessible, secure, and multifunctional. But it means that referring to specific features and controls in a book is asking for trouble because they will be out of date so quickly.

To address this tension between the vital nature of tech to the digital workspace with its rapid pace of change, I will instead maintain an online resource at healthyhappyhomeworking.com/tech, with links and recommendations. That way I can hopefully take account of changes and share the latest tools with you, without having to push out book updates every month.

Work first, tech second

The second reason though, is that it's easy to get distracted by the technology itself.

I know I do, there's nothing more likely to make me spin-off and stop working than spotting a tweet about a shiny new solution for this or that. Even if I'm not being paid to write about it I'll probably want to download it and play with it and feel seriously tempted to upend my life in order to accommodate it into my workflow because of one cool new feature I didn't even know I needed, and that is ridiculously unproductive and time-wasting.

It also reflects a problem even more profound than shiny object syndrome, which is the way that collaboration apps at work can lead to getting priorities upside down, letting the tail wag the dog, so to speak.

Instead, it's vitally important to think about exactly what *you* want the tool to do, what workflow or activity you want to create and support, and *then* go out and find the right tool — the best tool, or combination of tools — that delivers.

Don't get distracted by the bells and whistles in the slick two-minute explainer video that will make you wonder how you ever managed without this amazing thing in your life. They spent a good chunk of their marketing budget on that enticing animation, which is working exactly as intended — to drive downloads and satisfy those early phase investors with big numbers fast.

"But the trial is FREEEE", I hear you cry… Nope, step away from the download button. You'll thank me in the long run.

Sure, it's free to install, but the only way to test it properly with your own work will be to spend hours and hours setting it up, entering data, and in most cases finding that you subtly tweak what you're doing and how to fit the shiny new function you didn't even know you needed anyway but how cool *IS* that…?! And before you know it, you're trying to evangelise others to get on board and adopt the new shiny thing. Then your whole team or organisation is transitioning and battling to adapt their established routines to do things the new way, with the consequent lost productivity through the inevitable learning curve.

When the end of the free trial rolls around, the buyer's remorse is intense, because while you haven't spent money, you have committed huge amounts of time and effort — and may not have realised a shred of productivity gain even over the long term.

But the new app will do OK. Until you spot the next new shiny thing on Product Hunt or a press release.

Hey everyone, we have to check *this* out...

Staying up to date

Yes, you do need to review your tool stack from time to time and make sure you're using the best combination of apps which support the way you work. Occasionally something truly revolutionary comes along, and I'll be sure to tell you about it via social media or email (see below to sign up), however, for the most part, it's a case of new tools adding to a category with incremental improvement. It's worth trying to think like a master craftsperson — is this tool truly good enough to replace the one I've been using? Would I discard the tried-and-tested, in favour of it, without regret?

It could be that shiny one is now the best in breed which wasn't beforehand, but more likely it just means it's slightly better for some specific niche that might suit some user more than another for the time being. Anyway, I'll try to keep that section updated, and will welcome your feedback too. I hope we can grow a valuable community around the Healthy Happy Homeworking concept, and share whatever we learn.

Conclusion: So now what?

Whether by contrivance or consent, you're now part of the homeworker revolution, so welcome aboard. You've got some home-based work to do, and tools to help you establish somewhere safe and comfortable to do it.

I hope that this introduction to how to do homeworking the healthy happy way has been helpful, but this book is only the first edition of the first volume — because I wanted you to have it in your hands/on your device of choice as quickly as possible, and start benefiting from it.

I will do the same with the forthcoming books in the series, which will include:

- ☐ **Defining and protecting your boundaries when working from home**
- ☐ **Managing your time and attention when working from home**
- ☐ **Overcoming isolation while working from home**
- ☐ **From meetings to managers, being present when working from home**
- ☐ **Staying sane and healthy while working from home**

Please sign up at http://healthyhappyhomeworking.com/admin/ to receive updates on forthcoming releases, and updates from the community, on an occasional basis. You can follow us on Twitter @hhhomeworking too, and Instagram @healthyhappyhomeworking. We also have a supportive and welcoming Facebook community growing at https://www.facebook.com/groups/healthyhappyhomeworking, and we'd love to meet you there.

My firm intention is to create the content that YOU want to see, to help you in your own path to **healthy happy homeworking**, so I invite and genuinely welcome your input and feedback. Tell me what interests you, worries you, excites you, concerns you, or delights you, about working from home.

Thanks for reading.

Acknowledgements

Working from home is by definition a deeply solitary experience — nevertheless, it does not occur in a vacuum, and it's always important to recognise first and foremost the impact it has on one's closest family.

My deepest thanks must go therefore to Richard and the girls, whose lives have always been shaped by the way I do what I do, in ways which go beyond never having a dedicated spare bedroom. I believe the children of homeworking parents grow up with a unique perspective on work and the connection between effort and reward, but it inevitably means the work impacts on their lives and vice versa.

I am grateful too to all the people I have worked with and for over the years, at Saros and BlockSparks, who have been part of my remote work journey — including figuring out a lot of it the hard way. I particularly appreciate the diverse and interesting range of clients I presently work for, who keep me on my toes and growing professionally, while never having a chance to get bored (and still enabling me to squeeze in passion projects like this book). I must single out for special mention however Pilar Orti, director of Virtual Not Distant, who has not only been my longest-standing client as a freelancer but from whom I have learned so much about team dynamics and virtual consultancy.

Thanks to Tracy at Freshly Press, and Diana at Social Butterfly, for all their help in bringing this book to birth, along with the growing social presence around it. To Bex and Pilar for input as beta readers, and to everybody who is part of the Healthy Happy Homeworking community — from whom you will hear a lot more in subsequent books.

About the author

Following an early career in community development and voluntary sector training and facilitation in her native London, Maya transitioned to full-time home-based working at the turn of the millennium, by founding a market research fieldwork agency. While few resources were available at the time, she taught herself to develop and manage what turned out to be a fully remote team, in an era when this was still very unusual — and when the communications and collaboration technology infrastructure seemed prehistoric, compared to the present day.

As her team grew and remote team management practices evolved, she relocated to the Spanish Costa Blanca in 2009, in pursuit of a healthier and happier lifestyle for her young family. She ended up writing a tech and social media column for the local English newspaper, and has been freelancing full-time since 2017 — as an author, journalist and podcaster, now settled in Valencia on the Eastern coast of Spain.

In 2018 she became an e-resident of Estonia, and since then, trades as BlockSparks OÜ, telling the stories of the social impact of technology and future trends, following her passion for the tools and practices which enable people to live and work and thrive, wherever they choose.

She writes about subjects ranging from collaboration platforms to cryptocurrency, and writes and podcasts regularly for London-based remote work consultancy Virtual Not Distant, as well as writing for UC Today, and a range of other publications. She has written a novel about bitcoin, Beyond The Chain, and also co-authored Thinking Remote: Inspiration for Leaders of Distributed Teams.

Despite her passion for technology, Maya is also a big fan of unplugging from all of it from time to time and immersing herself in the joys of travel, hiking, culture, yoga, and all that her chosen Spanish home has to offer. So if she's not at her desk you'll find her on the beach or up a mountain, where all her best creative ideas seem to come to her.

www.ingramcontent.com/pod-product-compliance
Lightning Source LLC
Chambersburg PA
CBHW070425220526
45466CB00004B/1541